Victorian Britain

Jane Shuter

Adam Hook

HEINEMANN
EDUCATIONAL

Heinemann Educational
a division of Heinemann Educational Books Ltd
Halley Court, Jordan Hill, Oxford OX2 8EJ

OXFORD LONDON EDINBURGH MADRID
ATHENS BOLOGNA PARIS MELBOURNE
SYDNEY AUCKLAND SINGAPORE TOKYO
IBADAN NAIROBI HARARE GABORONE
PORTSMOUTH NH (USA)

First published 1992

93 94 95   12 11 10 9 8 7 6 5 4 3 2

**British Library Cataloguing in Publication
Data** is available from the British Library on
request.

ISBN 0 435 31809 8

Designed by Ron Kamen, Green Door Design
Ltd, Basingstoke, Hants

Printed in Spain by Mateu Cromo

Acknowledgements
The authors and publisher would like to thank
the following for permission to reproduce
photographs:

Birmingham Museum and Art Gallery: 2.6B,
3.4E
© The Board of Trustees of the Victoria and
Albert Museum: 1.2A, 2.5B, 2.6E, 2.7F
Bridgeman Art Library/Royal Holloway and
Bedford New College: 2.6A
Bridgeman Art Library/Wolverhapton Art
Gallery, Staffs: 2.8C
British Library: 2.7A, 2.7N
E. T. Archive: 2.5A
Greater London Photograph Library: 3.2C, 3.3D
Guildhall Library, Corporation of London: 3.5B
Guildhall Library, Corporation of
London/Bridgeman Art Library: 1.1E, 2.5D,
2.5G, 2.5I, 2.9A, 2.9B, 2.9C
Sonia Halliday Photographs/FHC Birch: 1.1C
Hulton-Deutsch Collection/Hulton Picture
Company: 2.7D
Illustrated London News Picture Library: 2.6G,
3.5D
Manchester City Art Gallery: 1.2D, 2.3C
Mansell Collection: 3.4C, 3.1C, 3.3I
Museum of London: 3.5C
© Museum of Science and Industry in
Manchester: 2.2A
© National Trust 1992: 2.2D
Oxfordshire Photographic Archive: 3.1E
Punch Photo Library: 2.4K
Reading Museum of Rural Life © University of
Reading: 2.2B
Adam Reich/Courtesy of Daniel Wolf, Inc, New
York: 3.4F
Royal Collection, St James's Palace © Her
Majesty the Queen: 2.7H
Sheffield City Museum: 2.4H
Tate Gallery: 3.2B
Tate Gallery/John Webb: 2.6C
Windsor Castle, Royal Library © 1992 Her
Majesty the Queen: 2.1D
Witt Library, Courtauld Institute: 2.4L
Derek Witty/Christ's Hospital, Horsham: 1.1A

Cover illustration: Crystal Palace, near Prince's
Gate. Lithograph by Brannan (Guildhall Library,
Corporation of London/Bridgeman Art Library).

Every effort has been made to contact copyright
holders of material reproduced in this book. Any
omissions will be rectified in subsequent
printings if notice is given to the publisher.

Details of written sources
In some sources the wording or sentence
structure has been simplified to ensure that the
source is accessible.

Sir Robert Ensor, *England 1870–1914*, Oxford,
1968: 3.3A
Pauline Gregg, *A Social and Economic History of
Britain 1760–1972*, Harrap, 1973: 2.3D
Eric de Maré, *London 1851, The Year of the Great
Exhibition*, Folio Society, 1972: 2.6F
Harold Perkin, *The Origins of Modern Society
1780–1800*, Routledge and Kegan Paul, 1969:
1.2B
L. C. B. Seaman, *Life in Victorian London*,
Batsford, 1973: 2.6D

Contents

1.1 Who were the Victorians?

The Victorian period covers the reign of Queen Victoria, from 1837 to 1901. Queen Victoria's reign lasted sixty-four years. Look at the following sources.

Source A

Source B

If we had to sum up our age in a short phrase, it is 'the Mechanical Age'. Nothing is now done by hand. There is no end to machinery. We fight with simple Nature and, with our unbeatable engines, always win and prosper.

Source C

Source D

It was an age of discovery. People discovered new lands, like America. In 1662 the first British scientific society was set up. It studied everything. It saw anything as possible. Some members, like Newton, made discoveries that we would call 'scientific'. But many of its members were just as keen to work on how unicorn horns could be used as medicine.

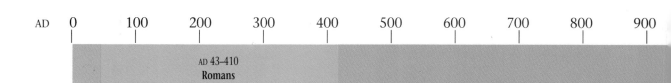

| AD | 0 | 100 | 200 | 300 | 400 | 500 | 600 | 700 | 800 | 900 |

AD 43–410
Romans

They wanted to keep people healthy. They had public baths and proper sewage disposal in towns. They carried fresh water into towns in huge aqueducts. They were not worried about inventing machines to work for them. They had plenty of slaves.

Were things different then?

1 Copy the three named periods on the timeline, each on a separate line. Next to each period write down the letter of the picture source and the written source that you think match the time period.

2 Write a sentence on each group, to explain why you matched them as you did.

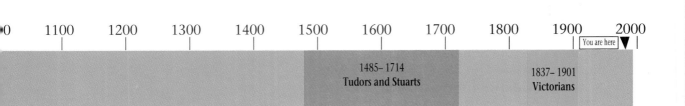

| 0 | 1100 | 1200 | 1300 | 1400 | 1500 | 1600 | 1700 | 1800 | 1900 | 2000 |

You are here ▼

1485– 1714
Tudors and Stuarts

1837– 1901
Victorians

1.2 Studying the Victorians

How do we find out about the Victorians? We can read books that have been written about them. We can also look at **sources** for **evidence** about what happened. Some sources from Victorian times are:

Written: like diaries, letters, newspapers, books, wills and government papers (for instance, laws and reports).

Pictorial: like paintings, cartoons and photographs.

Artefacts: actual objects made by people, like buildings or tools from the time.

Look at what the different sources on these pages tell us about how the Victorians felt about **class** (how society was organized, and how people thought everyone should behave).

Source A

A photograph of tea-time in a London garden. The photograph was posed, because early photographs took a long time to take. Photography was a new process in Victorian times, and gives us a new type of source.

Source B

As towns grew they became more organized. There were shops and offices in the centre. The factories and poorest working class areas were next to each other. Craftworkers (people who had special skills) and office workers lived further out. The middle classes lived in bigger houses on the outskirts of the town. The rich lived in the country, on their estates, although they might also have had a house in town.

Written by Professor Harold Perkin, a modern historian, in 1969. Historians look at lots of evidence from the time, and sum up what they have discovered.

Activity

Copy and fill in the following table for all of the sources in this unit. Put a ✔ under the column(s) that best describes the source.

Source	Written	Pictorial	Artefact
Source A			

Source C

Two nations who have no contact or sympathy, who know as little of each other's habits, thoughts and feelings as if they lived on different planets. They have been bred differently, fed on different food. They have different manners and are not governed by the same laws.

Written in 1846 by Benjamin Disraeli, who later became Prime Minister. He wrote this in a novel called 'Sybil'. He saw the rich and the poor as two different nations. We need to remember that novels were written to be read by other people.

How do we know?

1 Which people did most of the work in Victorian Britain?

2 How can you tell the difference between the classes in the picture sources?

3 Which source best shows that different classes behaved differently in Victorian times? Explain your answer.

Source D

'Work', painted in 1856 by Ford Madox Brown. Victorian painters took great care to get the details right in their paintings – for example the clothes, buildings, furniture and even the hairstyles. But they also wanted to sell their paintings. Even when the picture was meant to show bad conditions, it could not be too realistic. People seldom look really dirty, ugly or underfed.

2.1 Whose idea was the Great Exhibition?

1851 was a special year for the Victorians. The **Great Exhibition** was held in London. By studying the Great Exhibition we can find out a lot about Victorian people and how they lived.

Many people helped to pay for the Great Exhibition. They did this because they wanted to show that British-made **goods** were best, and also to make money from it. Many people went to the Great Exhibition. But whose idea was it?

Henry Cole, a member of the Society for the Encouragement of Arts, Manufactures and Commerce, was probably the first to suggest holding the Great Exhibition. He had seen a smaller exhibition in France in 1849. After that, he had organized several small exhibitions of British goods. He thought that the Great Exhibition would be a boost for British trade. Queen Victoria's husband, Prince Albert, was President of the same society. Albert liked the idea, and made speeches supporting it. He thought that the Exhibition would show how far all nations had progressed, and that it would be a starting point for further progress. Soon everyone was saying that it was Albert's idea.

Source A

Paxton's Crystal Palace was built for £80,000. It was a remarkable building. The idea of the Exhibition had, indeed, been Prince Albert's. He chose the site, and he was President of the Royal Commission which planned it.

Written by a modern historian.

Source B

The tremendous cheers, the joy on every face, and all due to my husband, the author of this 'Peace Festival' which united the industry and art of all nations.

Written by Queen Victoria, in her diary, on the day she opened the Great Exhibition.

Source C

Whoever had the first idea of the Exhibition it was the support of Prince Albert that made it a success. It was his enthusiasm that persuaded many people to give money and lend exhibits.

Written by a modern historian.

What do people say about the past?

1 Write down a **fact** and a **point of view** from Source A. Explain your choice.

2 Which other sources in this unit do you think the author of Source A might have used? Explain your answer.

3 Most people think that the Great Exhibition was Prince Albert's idea. Actually, it was probably Henry Cole's idea.

Why do you think most people believe that it was Prince Albert who thought of it?

This painting shows Queen Victoria giving a statue of Prince Albert to the town of Coburg, where he was born. She did this after his death in 1861. Albert is holding the plans for the Great Exhibition.

2.2 The Industrial Age

Victorian Britain made a lot of money from trade. The **factory owners** (the people who made the trade goods) needed to make a lot of goods as cheaply as possible. To do this they used and improved machines that had been invented before Victoria became Queen. The machinery helped produce more goods, but something had to work the machinery. The old ways (using horses, wind or water) were not very reliable. Steam power was used instead. People saw that steam could work many machines. These machines were quicker than people. The manufacturers put the machines in **factories**, so all the work was done in one place.

By the middle of the nineteenth century Britain was selling more goods than any other country. People called Britain 'the workshop of the world'.

Source A

A water-powered spinning frame, invented by Richard Arkwright in 1768. Many of these were joined together in the factories, to make long rows of spinning machines. Later, steam power made them even more efficient.

Steam was used in farming as well. It was resented there because it did the work of men, women and children. It meant harder work for those who could still get work.

Source B

A steam engine with the strength of 880 men can work 50,000 spindles. All this needs only 750 workers, to make as much yarn as 200,000 men did before.

Written in 1835 by Edward Baines, in 'A History of the Cotton Manufacture in Great Britain'.

Activity

Imagine steam power is coming to:
    a farm
    OR
    a cloth-weaving business.

Design two posters.
    The first should put the points in favour of steam power.
    The second should put the points against it.

Steam engines were soon powering factories and machines on a large scale. Notice the uses for steam in this picture. It is powering the furnace the men are working at, too.

Factory owners needed cheap **labour** (workers), as well as machines and steam power. Children were the cheapest to employ, because they were paid the lowest wages. In many families the parents could not get work in the factories. The only workers in the family were the children. This continued until the **Factory Acts** were passed, which stopped very young children working in factories.

Source F

Employers prefer to hire women or children, because they are cheaper. In the Lancashire mills average male wages are as follows:

Age 11–16   4s 10 $\frac{3}{4}$d a week.
Age 16–21   10s 2 $\frac{1}{2}$d a week.
Age 21–26   17s 2 $\frac{1}{2}$d a week.

The wages go even higher. So men are only employed to do the work that needs great strength or skill, or in a job that you could only trust a man to do.

Written in 1835 in a book about how the factory system worked.

A modern artist's idea of what it was like to work in the textile mills.

Source E

My girls work, I can find none. When the mills are busy they work from three in the morning 'til ten or half-past ten at night. They have two quarter-hour breaks, and half an hour for dinner. We dress them while they sleep standing up before we get them off to work. They are so tired towards the end of the working day that they have to be beaten to keep them awake. When they get home they are so tired that they fall asleep with their supper still in their mouths.

The father of two girl mill workers, describing his daughters' working day. He was talking to a committee set up to look at the working conditions of children in 1830.

Why did things happen?

1 A **cause** is something that makes things happen. What causes can you think of for Britain becoming such an important trading country by 1850? Give as many as you can.

2 There are different sorts of causes. **Enabling** causes **have** to happen first before other things can happen. Other causes just speed up what would have happened anyway. Which of the causes you have listed are **enabling** causes? Explain your choice(s).

3 A **consequence** is a result. Children were the cheapest people to employ in factories. What were the consequences of this?

2.3 Did factory work get easier?

To keep costs down, the factory owners paid low wages and spent very little on making factories safe. To begin with the government did little to change this. Official reports showed conditions were bad in factories. But it took a long time to pass laws which made things better. Each law was argued about. This was partly because some of the people who made the laws were also the people who ran the factories.

It was also because the Victorians believed that the government should not interfere in the way that people lived, even to help them. It was not until some people changed this view that laws were passed that really improved conditions. Even then, there was a big difference between passing laws and making sure that people obeyed them.

Source A

Cotton-spinners work in a heat of 80–84°F. They are locked in, except for half an hour at tea-time. They cannot send for water to drink, despite the heat. Then there is the dust and fuzz (cotton bits), which they breathe in. Men are aged by it; they cannot work after 50 years of age. Children are deformed and made ill.

Written in 1824 by William Cobbett, a man who was very keen on making the conditions of the workers better.

Factory Acts

1819: No child under 9 to work in cotton mills. Those under 16 could only work 12 hours a day.

1833: Children aged 9–13 could only work 9 hours a day. They should have 2 hours a day at school. Children aged 13–16 should only work 12 hours a day. No one under 18 could work through the night. From now on government inspectors were sent to check the Factory Acts were being carried out.

1844: Children could start work aged 8. From 8–13 they could only work for 6.5 hours a day, with a half day of school. Women and boys under 18 could only work for 12 hours a day. Dangerous machines should be fenced in.

1847: Women and all children under 18 could only work 10 hours a day, at any time.

1850: Women and all children under 18 could only work 10.5 hours a day and not at night.

1867: All factory workers on a 10 hour day.

Source B

Accidents happen because the machinery is seldom properly fenced in. Clothes and hair are caught and dragged into the machinery.

From a government report on working conditions written in 1842.

'Dinner Hour, Wigan', painted in 1874 by Eyre Crowe. Notice the sex and the age of most of the workers. How healthy do they look?

Activities

1 a What type of source is Source C?
   b Do you think it is accurate? Explain your answer.

2 What might historians think about factory conditions if they only had Source C?

Source
D

Two more reform acts were passed in 1867. Neither worked effectively. The Factory Act had too many exceptions built into it. The Workshop Act was far too vague.

Written by P. Gregg, a modern historian, in 1973.

What do people say about the past?

1 Give a **fact** and a **point of view** from Source D.

Leon

Factory life got better. You only have to look at the laws to see that.

Jenny

Factory life probably didn't get all that much better. You only have to look at what people at the time said.

2 Why might Leon disagree with Jenny?

2.4 Victorian towns by 1851

London was the largest city in Britain in 1851. By the early years of Queen Victoria's reign more people than ever before were living in towns. London and the northern factory towns grew enormously.

London had some silk weaving, but not much other cloth-making. Much work centred on the river, especially at the docks. Dye and glue factories were also there. Many women worked as dressmakers, either for themselves or in large groups for an employer. There was also a lot of work in the printing trade, both books and newspapers. Much of the work in London was to do with providing food and transport for the people who lived there.

Source A

Source B

A report from Bethnal Green says that all of the people there are silk weavers. They do not move away, or find other work, because this is all they can do. They are a very close community. Most people are out of work. There are 1,100 of them in the Workhouse, five or six to a bed. The whole district is in a state of hopeless poverty. The only answer is work, and they can find none.

Written in 1832 by Lord Greville. People went to the Workhouse when they had no homes or work. Families could not stay together in the Workhouse. Men, women and children had to live separately.

A modern artist's idea of a typical London street in 1851. You can see that traffic jams are not just a modern problem. ▼

LONDON·BRIDGE·RYS
TO THE GREAT EXHIBITION 3
RED LION WALHAM GREEN
BANK
SLOANE ST PICCADILLY. CHA
PUTNEY
COME TO THE GREAT EXHIBITION

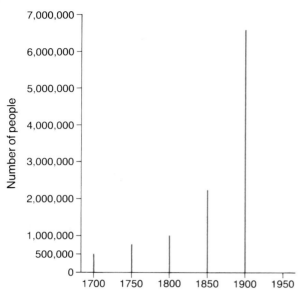

This graph shows how the population of
London grew. The figures for 1851 were
gathered by census. In a census, details
are taken about who lives in every house
in the country. The figures for 1700 and
1800 are rough estimates.

Activities

1 Look at Source A.
   Now look at all of the picture
   sources in the book. Which sources
   could the artist have used in order
   to do his painting? Explain how
   they support Source A.

2 Look at Source A.
   Imagine walking from one end of
   this street to the other. Write a
   description of everything that you
   can see, smell and hear.

For the first time ever there were towns that grew more quickly than London. Some of them were coal and iron towns, which grew with the industries that were already there. The fastest growing towns were the factory towns in the north of England. Before the factories came most of them had been much smaller.

The towns grew because they provided work. This meant that most of the people in the town were workers. People came to the towns to find work because they could find none in the country, and because pay was higher in the towns.

Source E

It's hard when folk can find no work
Where they've been bred and born.
When I was young I always thought
I'd grind my bread from corn.
But I've been forced to work in town
So here's my Litany:
"From Hull and Halifax and Hell
Good Lord, deliver me".

From 'The Dalesman's Litany', a popular song at the time.

Source D

▼ How some towns grew.

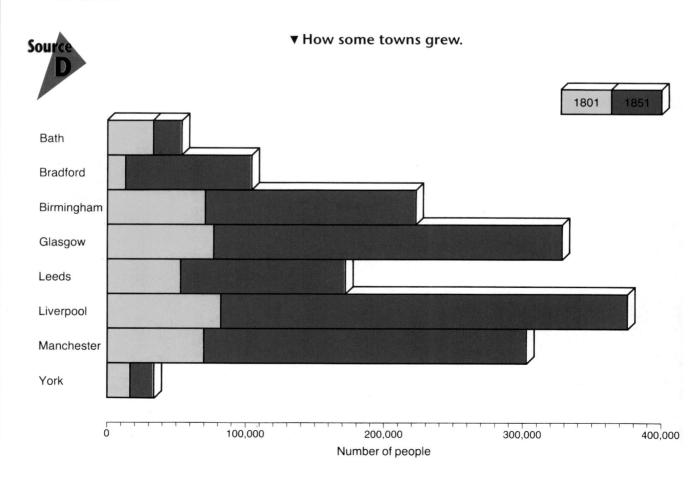

1801   1851

Bath
Bradford
Birmingham
Glasgow
Leeds
Liverpool
Manchester
York

0   100,000   200,000   300,000   400,000
Number of people

Source F

For many miles before they reached it they saw a grey cloud hanging over the town. They crossed the long, straight, hopeless streets of houses, all the same, all small. They had to stop constantly for wagons. Margaret had visited London, there had been several sorts of traffic there. Here every vehicle carried goods to do with cotton.

From 'North and South', a novel by Elizabeth Gaskell, published in 1854. She wrote several novels about the problems of Victorian life.

Source G

There are many Irish labourers in Manchester. They will work for very low wages. This keeps down the wages that the English workers can ask for.

Written by a Frenchman travelling in England at the time.

Activities

Look at Source D.

1 List the towns in order of how quickly they grew. Put the town that grew the most at the top of the list.

2 Write a letter from a farm labourer who has travelled to a factory town to work. Use the sources to help you. Say why you had to leave the countryside, what the town is like and why the wages were low.

Source H

The city of Sheffield, drawn in 1854.

The new houses for factory workers were built quickly, cheaply and badly. They were crammed full of workers and their families, sometimes as many as twenty people to a small room. Few houses had any water or toilets. Rubbish was often thrown into the river. Drinking water was often taken from that same river. This often made people ill. The most deadly illness was **cholera**.

From 1842 some people saw the link between the lack of clean water and cholera. There were reports like those for the factories which criticized living conditions in the towns. But nothing was done. Remember that the government disliked telling people what to do, even for their own good. But in 1848 there was a bad cholera outbreak. A **Public Health Act** was passed. It said that if there were a high number of cholera deaths councils could set up **Boards of Health** to raise money to improve their water supplies and the drains. Some towns, like Darlington, set up permanent Boards of Health, but most did not. The Act was so unpopular that it was not enforced after 1858, when it lost most of its power. It was not until 1866 that there were any more laws about public health.

 Source J

Average age of death	Manchester	Rutland
Professional/gentry	38	52
Tradesmen	20	41
Mechanics/labourers	17	38

The cost of building sewers, running water to the houses, and improving conditions would save on money lost through sickness and early death.

Written by Edwin Chadwick in a report to Parliament in 1842. Chadwick supported the idea of Boards of Health. His table compares a factory town (Manchester) with a town in the country (Rutland).

 Source K

THE WATER THAT JOHN DRINKS.

This is the water that John drinks.

This is the Thames with its cento of stink,
That supplies the water that John drinks.

These are the fish that float in the ink-
-y stream of the Thames with its cento of stink,
That supplies the water that John drinks

This is the sewer, from cesspool and sink,
That feeds the fish that float in the ink-
-y stream of the Thames with its cento of stink,
That supplies the water that John drinks.

A cartoon about the quality of London's water, published in 1849.

Source I

In Manchester everyone builds as they want. A row of houses may be badly drained, the streets may be full of pits of stagnant water, where people throw dead cats and dogs, yet no one may find fault.

From a report to Parliament, written in 1840.

Source L

'Children by a pond in Fulham', painted by C. Hunt in 1859. Are the boys taking any notice of the signboard? Who do you think put the sign up?

Source M

In this part of Liverpool the tap only works for a few hours each day. Everyone fetches as much water as they have pans to put it in. They have few pans, so they are often out of water.

Water collects in the pits in the broken ground. Dead dogs and cats are thrown into them, and other unmentionable things. Despite this, this water is used for cooking. I could not believe it.

Part of a report to Parliament, written in 1840.

Source N

In Inverness there are very few houses with toilets. Because of this there is not a street or a lane that is not filthy at all times. Sickness is seldom, if ever, absent.

From a report to Parliament on conditions in Inverness, written by Dr J. I. Nichol in 1842.

Were things different then?

Look back at the sources and activities in this unit.

1. Make a list of the things that were good and bad about living in towns if you were:
   a worker;
   a factory owner;
   a shopkeeper.

2. There has been a bad outbreak of cholera. A Board of Health is to be set up for your town. It will raise money from all but the poorest people to improve the drains and water supplies of the town. Say how this would affect you if you lived:
   in the slums;
   in a richer area.

   Try to think of good and bad effects.

2.5 How was the Great Exhibition put together?

The Great Exhibition nearly never took place. Not everyone thought it would help trade. They worried that big crowds would encourage crime. People argued over where it should be held. Prince Albert said it could be held in Hyde Park, but only temporarily. So the building had to be easy to take down. All the designs that were sent in seemed too solid. The committee produced its own design, using bits from all the others. Very few people liked it.

Joseph Paxton asked if he could suggest a design. He was told it had to be in quickly. His design was drawn up and accepted. It was different from all the others. Firstly, it used building parts of the same size and shape throughout so that they could be **mass produced**. Secondly, most of the building was made of glass. Paxton had built with iron and glass before, to make a big **glasshouse** (greenhouse). Until 1845 glass had been highly taxed, and expensive. It had only been used for glasshouses for the rich. Many people feared that the building would be unsafe. However, it would be easy to put it up and take down, and would not harm the park. The design was accepted.

Source A

One of the things people feared would happen when the crowds came to London. An early Victorian painting by J. O. Parry.

Source B

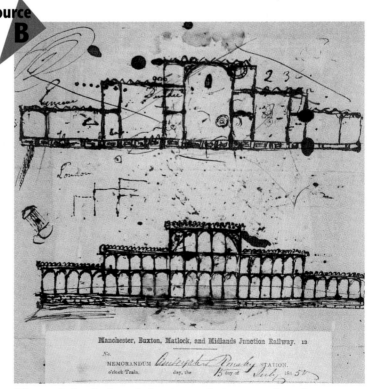

The original sketch by Joseph Paxton for the Crystal Palace. It was done on blotting paper, during a meeting.

Source
C

Some thought the whole building would tumble down, some that the noise of the cannons would shatter the glass. Many thought that the crowds would be intolerable, others that riots and rebellions would break out.

Written by Lady Charlotte Guest, the wife of an iron manufacturer, in her diary, on the day before the Great Exhibition opened.

Activities

1 Look at Source A.
What is happening in the picture?

2 Look at pages 22–23. Find as many reasons as you can that people gave for opposing the Great Exhibition.

3 Look at Sources B and D.
How was the design changed to keep the elm trees?

Source
D

The Crystal Palace. The design had to be changed so that three big elm trees could be left growing inside it.

People came to watch as the building went up. It survived the winter weather, including bad hailstorms. People who had been against it changed their minds. It was not falling down, and it looked splendid. It was nicknamed the **Crystal Palace**. The building was finished just fifteen months after it was decided to hold the Exhibition. It was completed so quickly because the parts used to build it were all a standard size, mass produced and easily put together. Also the parts were delivered quickly, by rail. The workmen had their jobs divided up so that each of them was doing a small part of the whole job, with as little wasted time as possible.

Source F

All sorts of jobs were going on at once: sawing, planing, glazing, painting, hammering, boarding. Steam curled from the little steam engines. Clouds of dust sprang up from the circular saws which were cutting the guttering to equal lengths. Machines guided loose gutters first through a trough of paint then through a gap fitted with brushes to take off the extra paint. One machine mixed putty, another cut lengths of wood. Cranes, wheels and pulleys were working everywhere.

From 'Tallis's History and Description of the Crystal Palace', written in 1851.

Source E

A modern artist's idea of what the building of the Crystal Palace was like.

Facts and figures

Workmen: In September 1850 there were 39 workers. By December there were over 2,000.

Iron: There were 1,060 iron columns, 2,224 girders, 358 roof supports and 30 miles of guttering.

Wood: They used 16,980 cubic metres of wood.

Glass: The men who put in the glass worked from trollies that slid along the gutters. Eighty men could fit 18,000 panes of glass a week.

Special effects: There was a boiler room with a steam engine to run the moving machinery exhibits. There was a complicated system of water piping that ran the fountains.

Visitors: On 25 February 1851 there were over 100,000 visitors, who paid 5s (25p) admission. The money was given to builders who were hurt while working on the building.

Activity

Imagine that you are either the lady or the gentleman (on the left of Source E) visiting the building of the Crystal Palace. Write a description of what you saw and heard for your diary. Perhaps you talked to the foreman. What did you ask? What did he say?

The Crystal Palace was a wonderful building, but for the Great Exhibition to be a success it needed to have exhibits from all over the world. This meant many countries had to work together, even countries that had recently been at war. There were over 100,000 objects, from over 5,000 different groups of people. Amazingly, everyone who sent exhibits managed to get them there on time except Russia, whose ships were stuck in icy seas. Delivery was helped by several new inventions.

Firstly there were **steam-powered ships**. When ships no longer had to rely on winds, they were able to time their journeys more accurately, and were therefore more reliable.

The second invention was the **telegraph**. This allowed people to send messages over long distances. It was much quicker to make arrangements by telegraph than by letter.

Source H

The progress of the human race, resulting from the common labour of all men, ought to be the final object produced by each individual. In helping this we are carrying out the will of God.

From a catalogue for the Great Exhibition.

▼ **The Tunisian bazaar (market) at the Great Exhibition. The tent is covered with lion skins.**

Source G

The Canadian part of the Great Exhibition. Canada was part of the growing British Empire.

Why did things happen?

1 Make a list of the causes which helped the Crystal Palace to be built on time.

2 Make a list of causes which meant that things arrived at the Great Exhibition on time.

3 There are many sorts of causes. **Political** causes involve relationships between groups of people or countries. **Technological** causes are to do with having the knowledge and equipment to make or do something. Put a **P** next to the causes on your lists that are political. Put a **T** next to the causes on your lists that are technological.

2.6 Getting there

Many people went to the Great Exhibition by train. The first railway ran from **Stockton to Darlington**, and was opened in 1825. After the **London to Manchester** railway was opened in 1830 everyone wanted to build railways. Many rail companies started up. Their railways had different track widths, and timetables that did not work together. Most companies had three classes of railway carriage: first, second and third. First-class carriages were very comfortable. Third-class carriages were little more than open wagons. Some had open sides but were roofed. The companies charged very different fares. All this made rail travel very difficult. In 1844 the government passed a **Railways Act** that made sure every company ran at least one train that stopped at every station each day. It set the third-class fare at 1d a mile. This made rail travel cheaper and easier.

Activities

1 When were Sources A and B painted?

2 What differences can you find between:
   the trains;
   the passengers?

3 What class of carriage do you think the passengers were travelling in?

Source A

'To Brighton and Back for 3s 6d',
painted in 1850 by Charles Rossiter.

'The Railway Station', painted
in 1862 by W. P. Frith. He
painted this using a set of
photographs of Paddington
Station, taken by a friend.

People travelling by road could travel by horse-drawn coach over long or short distances. They were crowded, uncomfortable and slow. Rich people had their own coaches. For short distances in towns people could hire small carriages, but these were expensive. It was in London, in 1829, that the first **omnibuses** were used. They were pulled by horses. They were cheaper than any other transport, but were still really too expensive for the poor. Poor people had to walk everywhere.

Source D

Most buses carried twelve passengers inside and three outside. Fares were 6d (2.6p) for short journeys, 1s (5p) for longer ones. Early buses had hard benches on either side, and straw covered floors. The conductors stood on a step at the back and tried to get people to use the bus – often by grabbing them and shoving them on! There were no fixed stopping places. Buses could be stopped anywhere, and could pick up from either side of the road.

Written by L. B. Seaman, a modern historian, in 'Life in Victorian London', 1973.

Source C

'Omnibus Life in London', painted in 1859 by W. M. Egley.

A cartoon drawn by the famous Victorian cartoonist
George Cruikshank. He called it '1851'. It is his idea
of what it was like at Picadilly Circus, the main
junction leading to the Great Exhibition in Hyde Park.

Activities

1 Look at Sources C and D.
   Think about a Victorian bus journey
   and describe it. How did you get
   on the bus? Was it comfortable?
   What did you see, hear and smell?

2 Look at Sources D and E.
   a How are people getting to the
     Great Exhibition in the cartoon?
   b Was the fare the same as usual?
   c Were the number of passengers
     riding on the roofs the same
     as usual?

How people travelled to the Great Exhibition depended on where they were coming from, how rich they were and how long they intended to stay.

If they were travelling a long way then they would probably start off with a train journey, unless they were rich enough to own their own carriages. If they were coming by train they might travel in first-class comfort, or they might come on the more uncomfortable and crowded **excursion** trains. Excursion trips also offered rooms in London for several nights as part of the fare.

Foreign visitors had to travel to England, before they got to London. As there were no aeroplanes, they would have had to travel by sea for at least part of the journey.

In London itself you could walk to Hyde Park, or take a carriage or a bus. The roads were very crowded. Many people decided to travel by river to Hyde Park instead. This meant that the river was crowded too.

Source F

Some people walked to London along the empty country lanes. Mary Callinak, 85, walked from Penzance with a basket on her head. The Queen described her as 'a most hale old woman, who was almost crying from emotion when I looked at her'.

Written in 1973 by Eric de Maré, a modern historian, in 'London 1851'.

A picture from a London newspaper, drawn during the Great Exhibition.

Source G

June 12: We saw three whole parishes, Crowhurst, Linchfield and Landford, from Kent and Surrey (800 in number), go by walking in procession two by two, the men in smock frocks, with their wives looking so nice. It seems they joined a savings club to come to London, on the advice of the clergyman, to see the Exhibition. It only cost them 2s and 6d (12.5p).

Written by Queen Victoria in her diary in 1851.

Were things different then?

Look back over all the sources and activities in this unit.

1 Make a design for a wall poster showing the different ways that people could get to the Great Exhibition.

2 **a** Explain how you would have travelled to the Great Exhibition if you were:
   Lady Charlotte Guest;
   a London office worker;
   someone from a village in Scotland.

   b Which of these people would have found it easiest to travel to the Great Exhibition? Explain your answer.

3 **a** How would people have travelled before the bus and train were invented?

   b How would this have affected where they could go?

2.7 Who went to the Great Exhibition?

Who went: The Queen

The whole of the royal family enjoyed the Great Exhibition, not just Prince Albert. The Queen visited it almost every day for the first three months. She worked her way around all of the exhibits, and talked to many people.

Source **B**

This is one of the greatest and most glorious days of our lives. Upon the Crystal Palace the flags of every nation were flying. This peace festival is uniting the industry and art of all nations of the earth. It was a day to live forever.

Written by Queen Victoria in her diary, on the day that she opened the Great Exhibition, 1 May 1851.

Source **A**

Elevation.

Ground Plan.

These 'ideal homes' were designed by Prince Albert. They were supposed to be built and rented out to working people at 4s (20p) a week. They showed builders that they could build better homes for the poor and still make a profit. Even so, the only ones ever built were in Kensington, London, as part of the Exhibition.

Source **C**

Went to the machinery part, where we stayed for two hours. What used to be done by hand and used to take months is now done in a few instants by the most beautiful machinery. What was particularly interesting was a printing machine worked vertically – many sheets are printed, dried and everything done in a second. We saw the great hydraulic lever, moved by one man, by which the great tubular bridge at Bangor was raised. It is most wonderful. We came home at a quarter to twelve and I felt quite tired and exhausted, mentally exhausted.

Written by Queen Victoria in her diary, 1851.

Activities

1 Look at Source A and read the caption. If builders could build better homes for the poor and still make a profit, why do you think that they carried on building houses that crowded the poor together in bad conditions?

2 Many Victorians talked about machinery as 'beautiful'. Look at the picture of the machinery hall on page 5. Do you think the machinery is beautiful? What do you think made it beautiful to the Victorians?

3 What other evidence can you find from the sources that Queen Victoria was interested in mechanical things?

Source
D

A photograph of Queen Victoria and Prince Albert, taken in 1861. Queen Victoria was very interested in photography. She had many photographs taken of her family. One of her ladies-in-waiting said you could always distract her by talking about photographs and how they were taken.

Who went: Famous people

Charles Dickens was a novelist and edited a paper called *Household Words* which ran stories written by himself and writers like Elizabeth Gaskell. He also wrote articles in the paper about many things, mostly the conditions of the poorest people of London. He moved to Broadstairs, Kent, in May 1851, worried that if he stayed in London he would be visited by all sorts of people who wanted to meet him. He came back in the summer, and was shown around the Exhibition by Paxton. He was not very impressed.

Lewis Carroll, the author of *Alice in Wonderland*, was interested in the exhibits, but was put off by the size of the building and the crowds. As well as writing stories, Carroll was interested in photography. He was impressed by the speed with which photography was changing. This was making it much quicker and easier to take photographs.

Source F

The opening ceremony of the Great Exhibition. Only very important people were invited.

Source E

There is too much of it. I do not like sightseeing anyway. This was too many sights in one place!

Charles Dickens writing about his visit to the Great Exhibition.

Alfred Lord Tennyson, the poet, wrote about how splendid the building was, and how it brought all sorts of people together in the same place.

Lord Palmerston was in the government at the time as foreign minister (in charge of relations with other countries). He became Prime Minister in 1855.

… famous for a day

The Chinaman in the picture was not an important person at all. People thought he was. Lady Charlotte Guest wrote in her diary that he stood with the diplomats, and even had a long conversation with the Duke of Wellington. Everyone thought that he was a Chinese diplomat. In fact he was the owner of a Chinese boat which was moored nearby on the River Thames. To get publicity for his Chinese Entertainments, he spread the story of how he had fooled everyone. What he did was more shocking then than it would be today. The idea of someone stepping outside his or her 'class' and mixing with more important people was seen as scandalous.

Source G

The building itself is far more worth seeing than anything in it, though many of its contents are worthy of admiration. You ought to come over and take a look before it closes.

Written by Lord Palmerston to the British Ambassador in Paris, on the day after the Great Exhibition opened.

Who went: Excursions

Many people went to the Great Exhibition on excursions. These were special, cheap trips run by the railway companies. For the Great Exhibition many companies offered a ticket price that included one or more nights in rooms in London. As a result, they were more crowded than the usual trains.

It was at this time that the idea of excursion trips to places other than London really took hold. The tickets were cheap. Many middle class families, and some of the better off working class ones, were able to visit places that they had never been able to afford to travel to before. Trips to the seaside were very popular.

Source I

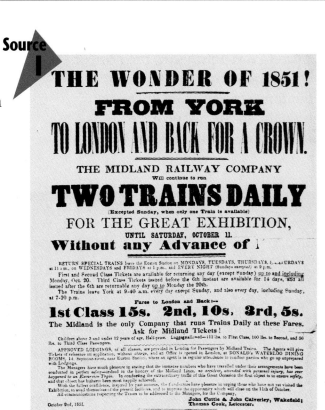

THE WONDER OF 1851!

FROM YORK

TO LONDON AND BACK FOR A CROWN.

THE MIDLAND RAILWAY COMPANY
Will continue to run

TWO TRAINS DAILY
(Excepted Sunday, when only one Train is available)
FOR THE GREAT EXHIBITION,
UNTIL SATURDAY, OCTOBER 11.
Without any Advance of F

RETURN SPECIAL TRAINS leave the Euston Station on MONDAYS, TUESDAYS, THURSDAYS, and SATURDAYS at 11 a.m., on WEDNESDAYS and FRIDAYS at 1 p.m., and EVERY NIGHT (Sundays excepted) at 9 p.m.

First and Second Class Tickets are available for returning any day (except Sunday) up to and including Monday, Oct. 20. Third Class Tickets issued before the 6th instant are available for 14 days, and all issued after the 6th are returnable any day up to Monday the 20th.

The Trains leave York at 9-40 a.m. every day except Sunday, and also every day, including Sunday, at 7-20 p.m.

Fares to London and Back:—

1st Class 15s. 2nd, 10s, 3rd, 5s.

The Midland is the only Company that runs Trains Daily at these Fares.
Ask for Midland Tickets!

Children above 3 and under 12 years of age, Half-price. Luggage allowed—112 lbs. to First Class, 100 lbs. to Second, and 56 lbs. to Third Class Passengers.

APPROVED LODGINGS, of all classes, are provided in London for Passengers by Midland Trains. The Agents will give Tickets of reference on application, without charge, and an Office is opened in London, at DONALD's WATERLOO DINING ROOMS, 14, Seymour-street, near Euston Station, where an agent is in regular attendance to conduct parties who go up unprepared with Lodgings.

The Managers have much pleasure in stating that immense numbers who have travelled under their arrangements have been conducted in perfect safety—indeed in the history of the Midland Lines, *no accident, attended with personal injury, has ever happened to an Excursion Train*. In conducting the extraordinary traffic of this Great Occasion the first object is to ensure *safety*, and that object has hitherto been most happily achieved.

With the fullest confidence, inspired by past success, the Conductors have pleasure in urging those who have not yet visited the Exhibition, to avail themselves of the present facilities, and to improve the opportunity which will close on the 11th of October.

All communications respecting the Trains to be addressed to the Managers, for the Company.

October 2nd, 1851. John Cuttle & John Calverley, Wakefield; Thomas Cook, Leicester.

T. COOK, PRINTER, 2s, GRANBY-STREET, LEICESTER.

A poster for an excursion trip.

Source H

The first real event of my life was in 1851, when I was six years old. My mother took me up to see the Great Exhibition. Our special Exhibition train from Thirsk to King's Cross was a wonder to me. The train was of enormous length and drawn by six locomotives. Every seat was occupied.

Written by R. E. Crompton in 1928. He later became an engineer because of his fascination with trains.

Dear Mr. Cook,
I wish it was in my power to tell you how much we owe you for these cheap excursions. Only think, for a few shillings I, a poor working man, have been able to see the glories of the fine old city of York that I could never have seen but for your special train from Nottingham today.

One of the first thank you letters written to the first British travel agent, Thomas Cook. He set up a company that ran excursions in Britain, and more expensive holidays abroad. There are still travel agencies that have his name today.

Activities

1 The author of Source K calls himself 'a poor working man'. What is there about his letter that makes you think that he was not one of the very poor?

2 Look at Source H. Draw a typical beach scene today. Make sure that you include people of all ages. If there are things happening in the picture that would still go on today (like digging in the sand) make sure that you put them into your picture.

'Ramsgate Sands', painted in 1851 by W. P. Frith.

Who went: Everyone!

It seemed to people at the time that everyone in Britain, and many foreigners too, went to the Great Exhibition. Cartoons and writings at the time all stressed how everyone could go and was going. Henry Mayhew and George Cruikshank, a famous journalist and cartoonist of the time, wrote a book called *1851: or the Adventures of Mr and Mrs Sandboys and Family who came up to London to Enjoy Themselves and to see the Great Exhibition*. The sources on this page are all extracts from this book.

Source L

Every city was arranging some 'monster train' to shoot the whole of its inhabitants, at a halfpenny a ton, into the lodging houses of London. Every village, hamlet, borough, township had its club collecting money to provide its inhabitants with a three day journey to London, a mattress under the arches of the Adelphi Theatre, and a ticket for as much soup as they could eat.

Source M

As the morning wore on the crowd got thicker and thicker, until it was a road of human heads. All London, half the country, and a good part of the world were on their way to see the Queen open THE GREAT EXHIBITION OF ALL NATIONS.

Source N

The landlady of the last lodging house with any room in the centre of London offers Mr and Mrs Sandboys a hammock to share in the corridor, for 5s (25p) a night. Their daughter and the maid can share the landlady's bed, while their son is offered the top of the grand piano.

This is

Activities

1 Look at Source N. Write the conversation between Mrs Sandboys and the landlady. Think what Mrs Sandboys might object to about what she was being offered, and the price. Think of the landlady's reply.

2 Read Source O. What do you notice about the things that people are interested in?

Looking for Lodgings.

ave ma'm: — I have just let the last tent on the tiles to a Foreign Nobleman

Source O

Here you see a railway guard hurrying towards the locomotive (train) department. Next you come to a carpenter, admiring a huge top carved from a mahogany tree. Among the agricultural instruments stroll groups of countrymen in smocks. The machinery has, from the first, been the main focus of attention. The chief centres of curiosity are the power looms. Around all the machines are workers, farmers, children all trying to work out how it all works.

How do we know?

You will need to look at all of the sources in this unit to answer the questions.

1 What kind of people went to the Great Exhibition?

2 Which source would you use if you wanted to show that:
   a The Exhibition was a great success?
   b The Exhibition was quite a success?
   c The Exhibition hardly mattered at all?

2.8 Who didn't go?

There were times when it seemed that everyone in the whole world went to the Great Exhibition at least once. Some people, for various reasons, did not go.

Many people did not go for **economic** reasons. They could not afford to go. The cost of getting in ranged from £1 to 1s. But there were many people who did not have enough money to feed themselves. They could not afford even 1s.

Then there were **political** reasons. The Exhibition was seen as uniting every country in the world, but that was not quite true. China did not send any exhibits because it was quarrelling with Britain over trade. The Chinese exhibits were collected from people on the organizing committee who had Chinese things in their homes to lend.

Some people did not go for **personal** reasons. Many people were scared of the idea of the crowds, others thought that it was too dangerous. Those who lived in the country may not even have heard about it. Other people were just too busy doing something else. Going to the Great Exhibition may not even have crossed their minds.

Source B

Edward Slack and his wife are both stocking makers. They have six girls and one boy. The most they can earn each week, with everyone working all day and into the night, is 12s 3d. His wife cannot earn as much when she is very pregnant. Weekly, they spend:

Rent	1s 8d
Coal	1s 0d
Candles	7d
Soap	4d
Bread	7s 7d
Potatoes	7d
Coffee	3d
Total	12s 0d

To buy clothes for the children they have to give up food. They seldom eat meat. They never eat cheese, butter or sugar. Even so they are not seen as really poor. They are charged 8s a year for the poor, and 2s a year to help mend the roads. They are behind on paying these.

Taken from an interview with a working family in 1842. The most they can possibly earn is 12s 6d a week. The least they can spend is 12s a week.

Source A

The Workhouse had some 1,500 to 2,000 paupers, ranging from the infant newly born to the old man dying on his bed. We walked for two hours around the building. Most people were unwilling to talk, and seemed to care for little besides warmth and food.

Written by Charles Dickens in 'Household Words', 1850. These people were poor and listless. Workhouses gave people work, food and shelter, but families were split up. Many families preferred to stay together, even if it meant no food and sleeping outside.

The family in this country cottage would not have had money to spare for the Great Exhibition. They may not even have heard about it.

In 1851, a plan was made to extend the country post service. I rode almost all over southern England to examine the postal networks, and set up proper ones. I did not write any books, I hardly saw my family. I had time for nothing else.

Written by Anthony Trollope in his autobiography. Trollope wrote novels, and worked for the post office. He must have heard of the Great Exhibition, but it made no impression on him. He does not talk about it at all.

Why did things happen?

1 Make a list of causes that explain why some people did not go to the Great Exhibition. Put each cause on a new line.

2 Put an **E** next to the causes that were economic, a **P** next to the ones that were political, and a **Pe** next to the ones that were personal.

3 Make a list of the sources in this unit. Next to each source, write the cause that best explains why the person or people in it would not have been to the Great Exhibition. If you can't be sure of a cause, or think it might be a mixture of causes, then explain this.

2.9 What did they see?

The most amazing thing about the Great Exhibition was the range of different things that were on show. There were big things, like the moving machinery. There were tiny things, like china ornaments. There were statues, toys and plants. There were useful things, like weaving looms or envelope folding machines. There were silly things, like the sportsman's penknife which had eighty blades and corkscrews, or an 'alarm bedstead' that could be set to catapult you into a cold bath when you woke up!

Source A

China sent from France. Britain made a lot of china, but not of such high quality. Queen Victoria liked this French china, and bought crates of it.

Source B

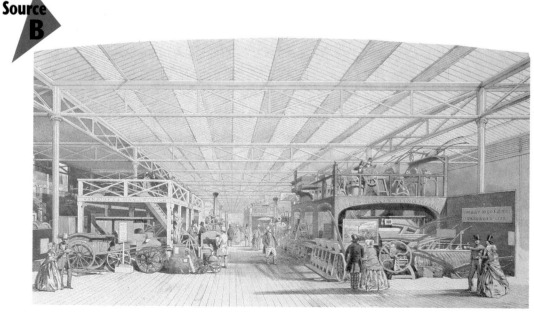

The farming machinery stand. This was supposed to be the first place that people from the country headed for.

Music was a very important form of Victorian entertainment.
These pianos were expensive ones, made for the homes of the
rich. But most middle class homes had a piano in their sitting
rooms, much smaller and plainer than these.

Some of the Exhibits

Beds	Carpets and rugs
Statues	Furniture
Vases	Stained glass
Material	Sledges
Fans	Coaches
Musical instruments	Food
Paintings	Stuffed animals
Toys	Mirrors
Plants	China
Machinery	Jewellery

The largest diamond in the world

'The Old Ways' (a display about the
middle ages, mostly of objects from
churches, including copies of tombs
and statues)

Models of docks, lighthouses and
railways

Oddly for a festival dedicated to peace,
there were guns and cannon.

How do we know?

Look at the sources on this page, and also
Source E on page 5, Source D on page 23,
Sources G and I on pages 26–7, Sources A
and C on page 34, Source F on pages
36–37 and Source O on page 41.

I Design a poster to show the range of
different things that could be seen at
the Great Exhibition. Make sure you
only use things you know were there.

2 Which source(s) would you use if you
wanted to show that the Great
Exhibition was concerned with:
a industry;
b everyday life?

Explain your answers.

3.1 Counting the people

You have seen that Victorian towns grew quickly. This was partly because people moved to the towns for work. It was also because the **population** (number of people) of Great Britain went up. In 1801 the first **census** of Britain was taken. On a particular day the people who were in every house in the country were listed. This has been done every ten years ever since except 1941. From 1851 onwards the information has included their ages, jobs and where people were born.

Historians disagree about how useful the census details are. Most agree that they give a good rough guide to population, jobs and family size. But there are many important things that they do not tell us, and there are arguments about how accurate they really are. These arguments were going on even at the time.

Source B

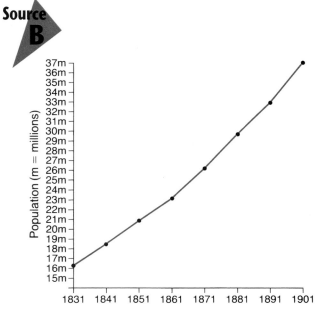

The census figures for the whole country from 1841 to 1901. Figures for the whole country show general population changes. They hide the fact that the population changed differently in different parts of the country.

Source A

A sample of the 1851 census form for Banbury, Oxfordshire, showing the information that was collected.

TAKING THE CENSUS.

The Victorian cartoonist George Cruikshank's view of the problems of collecting census information.

This great investigation is about to happen again, and will give totally false returns. We say false because the checks on who slept where on that night are wildly inefficient. The people unnumbered in the Census include waiters, tramps, gamblers, breakfast-stall keepers, steamboat workers and passengers, mail-train passengers, show people, lamp-lighters, and many famous people who seldom rest at night. These include the editor of *The Times*.

From the magazine 'Punch', 1851.

Activity

Read Source D and the box headed Who was **not** counted? Make up some people who might have missed being counted in a census taken today.

Who was **not** counted?

The magazine *Punch* discussed the problems of the time in a funny way. It said it was not possible to collect accurate census information. It invented some people who would not have been in the census at all:

Mr Mark Lane: a clerk. He went out to eat and drink, walked around for a bit, and finally slept on the table in his office.

Joseph Badger: a cabman. He spent all evening driving people from place to place. He slept in his cab from time to time.

Mr Gregory Barnes: a doctor. He spent all night rushing from place to place delivering babies and stitching up split skulls.

Here are some entries in the census for Parsons Street, Banbury, a street close to the centre of the town.

Parsons Street, 1851

George Parson	40	Hairdresser
Ann Layton	54	Housekeeper
William Humphries	19	Assistant
Carolyn Bayley	15	Servant
Robert Baxter	43	Bootmaker
Henrietta, wife	41	
William, son	21	Bootmaker
Amy, daughter	20	
John, son	13	Apprentice
Frederick, son	13	School
William Tarlton	33	Bootmaker
Edmund Saw	21	Bootmaker
Michael Husband	21	Bootmaker
Thomas Kingerlee	40	Plumber and glazier
Caroline, wife	43	
William, son	10	School
Thomas, son	8	School
Alfred, son	6	School
Marianne, daughter	3	
John Walshaw	48	Grocer
Hannah, wife	52	
Edward Payne	23	Shopman
William Page	25	Travelling assistant
Charles Hartwell	20	Assistant
Frederick Sellars	17	Apprentice
John Rattle	17	Servant
Liz Vause	26	Servant
Jane Yorke	27	Servant
Thomas Slatter	26	Butcher
Louisa, sister	23	Housekeeper
John Foster	16	Apprentice
James Prescott	46	Draper
Mary, sister	38	Housekeeper
Charles Harvey	25	Assistant
Anthony Smelt	23	Assistant
John Drake	17	Apprentice
Elizabeth Heritage	23	Servant
Richard Grimes	18	Servant
William Potts	51	Printer
Sarah, mother	81	
William, son	25	Reporter
John, son	20	Apprentice
Emma Grissold	20	Servant

Parsons Street, 1891

Frederick Dubleton	31	Bootmaker
Alice, wife	31	
Frederick, son	8	
Ernest, son	5	
Percival, son	3	
Elinor, daughter	2	
Nathaniel Bennett	77	Father-in-law
Lizzie Tew	14	Servant
Annie Green	12	Nurse
Alfred Kingerlee	46	Draper
Charlotte, wife	39	
George, son	15	
Ann Marks	24	Shop assistant
Liz Smith	24	Shop assistant
Sarah Smith	19	Servant
George Mould	55	Photographer
May, wife	60	
William Williams	63	Butcher
Sarah, wife	60	
Bernard, son	38	Butcher
John, son	30	Butcher
Ada, daughter	29	
Amos Tearle	56	Confectioner
Liz, wife	57	
Frederick, son	30	Theology student
Mary Essex	90	Mother-in-law
Henry Bryan	38	Hairdresser
Marsha, wife	39	
Charles, son	16	Outfitter's apprentice
Florence, daughter	7	
Mary Sevell	76	Visitor
Richard Potter	16	Apprentice
Eliza Blackwell	15	Servant
William Thompson	40	Cycle agent
Enid, wife	35	
William Dosset	33	Grocer
Alice, wife	25	
Gertrude, daughter	2 months	
Lucy Timms	17	Servant
William Woodhill	26	Greengrocer
Sarah, wife	25	
Maud, daughter	2	
Charles, son	2 months	
Emily Knighton	14	Servant
John Potts	60	Publisher
Sarah, wife	56	
Willian, son	22	Sub-editor
Kate, daughter	21	Art school student
Bessie, daughter	18	Art school student
Fred Speck	49	Brother-in-law, soldier

Part of Parsons Street, Banbury, in the early 1900s.

What did they do?

Draper: sold cloth and sewing things (needles, buttons and thread).

Bootmaker: made boots and shoes, and sometimes luggage too.

Clerk: worked in an office filing and writing letters and other documents.

Publisher: prepared books for the printer to print.

Grocer: sold food, not fruit or vegetables.

Glazier: worked with glass, usually for windows, but also greenhouses etc.

Cycle agent: sold bicycles.

How do we know?

1 Look at both census lists.
   a Which families are still there?
   b Who has moved?

2 Look at Source E and the census information for 1891.
   a Which shops and people from the census information can you find in the picture?
   b Who has moved? Why do you think this was?

3 What information would you need for a study of your town in Victorian times? Explain your choices.

3.2 School time!

Ideas about education changed in Victorian times. The idea grew that education should be for everyone, not just for the rich who could afford to pay. At the beginning of the period the government did little to help. There had been an **Education Act** in 1833 which gave government money to church schools. But it was not until 1870 that the government set up its own state schools, and made sure than everyone under ten years old went to them.

Source A

The school was in three of the most awful rooms on the first floor of a rotten house. The children were filthy and wild. I cannot see how they could have been taught anything in that place.

Written in 1843 by Charles Dickens, after a visit to a 'ragged school'. These were run to give the poor some education. In 1844, Lord Ashley was made president of the society that ran them. The schools got better. Ashley gave a lot of his money to the society. He even stopped MPs as they went into Parliament to ask them to give money!

Source B

A dame school (so called because many were run by ladies who could find no other work). This was the only education most children had in early Victorian times. The school in the picture is cleaner, better organized and less crowded than most were.

Exercise in a school playground. By the end of the Victorian period, schools had special buildings and their own outdoor space. There were proper classrooms, and desks where the children sat in rows.

Government and education

1833: Government money given to church schools. This was after the Factory Act said children had to have two hours schooling. Inspectors checked how the money was spent.

1846: A pupil-teacher system was set up. Older children taught the younger ones. This was after a new Factory Act sent more children to school.

1862: People felt that children were not learning enough. They set up 'standards'. The amount of money a school got depended on how many children in each class reached the 'standard'. Government inspectors were to carry out tests.

1870: New Education Act. The government set up state schools where no church schools existed. This followed the 1867 Act which gave working men the right to vote.

How did things change?

Look at the sources and the text.

1 How did the education of young children change between 1837 and 1901?

2 Do you think the changes were the same for all children, all over the country?

Activity

What made the government get more involved in education?

3.3 Life in late Victorian London

By 1901 the earlier divisions in society had become much more fixed **class** divisions. There was a basic division between upper, middle and lower classes. But each class had its own divisions. Not everyone in each class led exactly the same lives. We have described life in the middle of each group.

The **upper class** (the rich) lived in the country in large houses and often owned a lot of land. They came to London in summer, for what they called 'the Season'. There were balls, dinners, dances and entertainments all through the season. The main point of this was to arrange marriages for their children. They went abroad for holidays, at the same time as each other, and to the same places.

The upper class did not have to work. They often did charity work. The men might have had a seat in Parliament. They had servants to run their homes and land. They had maids to clean and serve the food and footmen and a butler to answer the door. They had cooks and kitchen servants. There were ladies' maids (or gentlemen's valets) to dress them and look after their clothes. Men worked in the gardens and the stables, collecting the rents and keeping out the poachers. The children had nannies and governesses and spent little time with their parents. They even ate in the nursery or the schoolroom most of the time.

Source A

William Cory, visiting Lord Northbrooke in his Hampshire country house recorded one day, not Sunday, in detail. At 9am the family, guests and all the servants were read a chapter of the Old Testament, and prayed together. This is not recorded as unusual. It is thought to have been usual practice until the late 1880s.

Written by Sir Robert Ensor, a modern historian. Almost everyone went to church on Sunday, often more than once. Religion was important. Upper class people were more likely to belong to the Church of England.

Source B

At Belvoir there were many servants. There was an old man whose job was just to bang the gong for lunch, at the time to change clothes for dinner, and for dinner. Every corridor had to be warmed, and I suppose it must have taken well over ten minutes to tour the visitors' rooms. There were also men who spent all their time carrying hot water for baths, and others who spent all of their day changing the candles.

Written by a lady about her childhood in an upper class home in the late 1880s.

Activity

Imagine you had servants to do everything for you. What would you do all day?

Source
C
A modern artist's impression of an upper class dining room in the 1890s.

By 1901 there were many more **middle class** families than there had been in 1837. They were mostly better off in 1901. The men were either 'professional' (doctors, lawyers, bankers) or well-off tradesmen. Their wives did not go out to work much, although some might help in the family business. They had at least one servant, often more. A usual number of servants would be a cook, a maid, a gardener and a coachman. They saw more of their children, because their homes were smaller and their lives were less formal. They were more likely to spend the evening together, listening to father reading or one of the girls playing the piano.

Some adventurous middle class people started to go on holiday abroad at this time. Travel companies, like the one set up by Thomas Cook, were making foreign travel cheaper.

Church going was most important to the middle class. Some belonged to the Church of England, but others joined churches that worshipped in a different way. Whatever church they went to, they believed in God and prayed regularly. Many families had morning prayers, which the servants also had to go to.

Source D

A middle class London home in Cheyne Walk. The eldest daughter of the Marshalls, who lived in this house in the 1880s, left a diary which is mostly concerned with finding a husband.

Source E

Mr Brown is really very pleasing. Still, he may come once and never again.

Papa is concerned about Mr Brown, and thinks there must be a reason for his silence. I begin to forget him. I can't help feeling that he did care for me. However it is all past and gone and I shall never marry *now*.

It has been a horrid year. Mr Brown has vanished utterly, A. D. only seen once, for an instant. Mr Cartwright is also invisible again.

Entries from Jeanette Marshall's diary for 1879–80. Jeanette did eventually marry a Dr Seaton in 1891. She was 33, and he was 43. The details of their courtship are also in her diary.

Source F

A modern artist's impression of a
middle class dining room in the 1890s.

Everyone in a **working class** family worked, unless they were too young to do anything. They worked as much as they could. Life was one long struggle to find enough money to live. They often lived in one room, although lucky people had more rooms. For many working class people, especially in London and the northern towns, life was not much better in 1901 than it had been in 1837.

There were few holidays. Some people went to Kent in the summer, to work in the hop fields. The work was hard, and the living conditions were bad. But at least they were out in the fresh air for a change. The only other holiday that they might, very occasionally, afford was a day's excursion on the train, preferably to the seaside.

Source H

We lived in a three roomed house. It backed on to another house. The space between them had a six-seat earth toilet that we all used. Our bedroom was right over this. The smell was vile; we had to keep the window open all year. We had no bedding. We slept on straw, under coats and sacks.

Written by Jack Lanigan, about Salford in the 1890s.

Source I

Late Victorian working class housing. Notice how drainage and fresh water are provided.

Source G

We didn't go to church. My mum had no time. Matt and I never went to Sunday school, because we had no decent clothes. We went to Gravel Lane Ragged (Sunday) School, where everyone was as bad off as us and all barefoot.

Written by Jack Lanigan, about growing up in Salford in the 1890s.

Were things different then?

Life was not the same for everyone in late Victorian times. Would you rather have been:
upper class;
middle class;
or working class?

Think about the good and bad points of each life. Use this unit to help explain your reasons.

A modern artist's idea of a working class dining room in the 1890s.

3.4 The British Empire

Between 1837 and 1901 the British Empire (all the countries controlled by Britain) grew. These countries were often called **the colonies**. Some colonies had few British people living in them, mostly the people who had been sent to run them. Others had many British people living there, who **emigrated** (moved) to find a better life. Many British people emigrated in this period. Many Irish people emigrated because of a bad **famine** (food shortage) that swept the country. Some emigrants went to America, but many went to the colonies because they got help to pay for moving there. In the south of England, where there was most unemployment, people set up committees to help pay for the poor to emigrate. It was cheaper than paying for them to be looked after in workhouses. The Australian government offered free crossings to 'suitable' families. They were not paying for the poor, like the British committees. They wanted people who had useful skills.

One such emigrant was **William Webb**. He was born in a Wiltshire village in 1830. Webb and two of his older brothers became engineers. There was no work for them in their village. Each of them moved to a town to train as soon as they were old enough. Webb's oldest brother emigrated to America. Later Webb and his other brother emigrated to Australia. The written sources on this page are from Webb's autobiography, written in the 1880s.

Source A

Country life at the time was very miserable. Wheat was scarce and dear. We had to use barley flour, which made bad bread. People were often ill. Most people could not find work. Many of those who had work were often sick too.

Source B

My eldest brother Maurice had emigrated to Texas, USA. My next eldest brother, Henry, was an engineer in Exeter. He suggested emigrating to Australia, where gold had just been found. The Australian Government was giving money to pay for working men and their families to emigrate. We hoped to make a better life for ourselves, but there were many who went just for the gold. My brother took his wife and four sons with him.

Source C

A Victorian artist's impression of conditions on board an emigrant ship, drawn in 1887.

We sailed from Plymouth on *The Prian* in May 1852. We were on board for 96 days. Our first sight of Australia was at Portland Bay. We asked about Melbourne, the next port (many days' sail away). Most of us passengers decided to stay in Portland. Most of the men were away digging for gold at Ballarat. We found an empty house and land quickly. We got some flour and a camp oven and set up home.

Activities

1 **a** How long did it take Webb and his relations to sail to Australia?
   b Why do you think that most passengers decided not to travel on to Melbourne?

2 Write a letter from Webb to his parents, explaining why he and Henry have decided to emigrate.

3 Draw a bar graph using the figures below to show how many people emigrated from Britain. Why do you think so many people were emigrating?

1820–29	216,000
1830–39	668,000
1840–49	1,495,000

'The Last of England' painted by Ford Madox Brown in about 1850. The journey is being presented as an adventure. The passengers on the ship seem very healthy and well dressed. The boat is called 'Eldorado', a name given to a fairy-story city of gold. The lady is holding a baby under her cloak, you can just see its hand.

The Victorians were very proud of their Empire. They were pleased that they had so many countries under their control. This was not just because it made them feel important. The more colonies they had, the more countries they could trade with on terms that were good for Britain. Also, if a country was part of the Empire, it could be used as a base from which to add more countries and trading partners to the Empire.

In all parts of the Empire the British took very little notice of the ways of the people who were already living there. British rules and ways of life were brought in.

How did things change?

1 How did the British Empire change between 1837 and 1901? Explain your answer.

2 Would you say that this change was **rapid** (quick) or **gradual** (slow)?

Britain also traded with countries that were not part of the Empire. These businessmen are in a mat and basket factory in China. Most British traders who lived abroad behaved like the English colonists. They tended to live in the same areas, and behave as if they were still in Britain. They did not change the type of clothes they wore or their eating habits. Very few of them learnt the language of the country they lived in. ▶

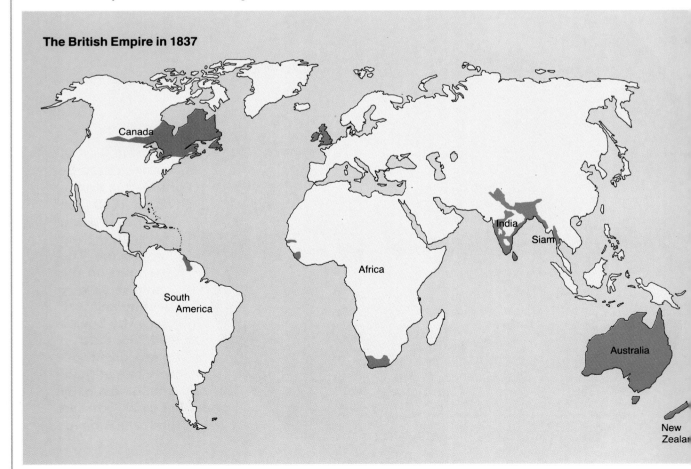

The British Empire in 1837

Canada

India

Siam

Africa

South America

Australia

New Zealand

Source F

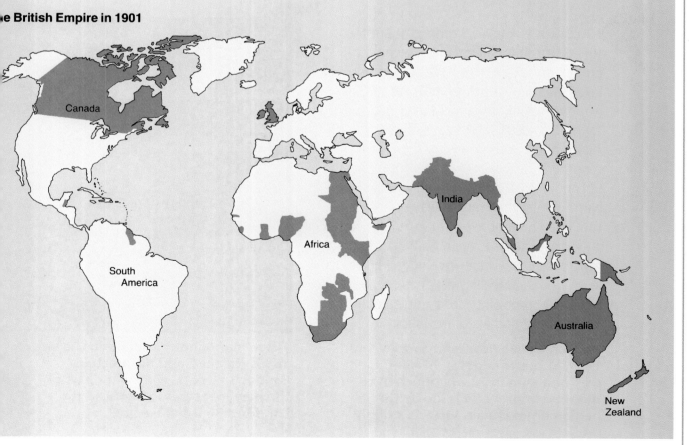

e British Empire in 1901

3.5 Had things changed?

Between 1837 and 1901 many things changed in Britain. By the time Queen Victoria died the country looked very different. People had built bridges, railways, stations, schools, town halls, museums, factories, houses and sewage works. People were different. Most people had had some basic education. They moved around the country more. But not everything was better. There was still a big gap between rich and poor people. Ideas about class split people up even more.

Discoveries and inventions

	Invented	Significant use
The typewriter	1851	1880
Telephone	1876	1901
Telegraph	1837	1870
Photography	1839	
box camera	1880	1901
Cinema	1895	1901
Underground		
railway system	1863	1900 (London)
Bicycles	1879	1901
Electricity	1831	1926

(In 1878, 30,000 people watched a football match in Sheffield lit by huge electric lamps.)

Source A

Gas was unknown. I groped about the streets of London in darkness, with no protection except an old watchman. It could take nine hours to sail from Dover to Calais without steam, the same time to go from Taunton to Bath before the railroads. Now Taunton to London only takes six hours. I can, thanks to the police, walk from one end of London to another without coming to harm. If I get tired on the way I can take a cab. I had no umbrella! They were little used and very expensive. I had no braces to hold my trousers up. There were no medicines for fever, gout and feeling sick. I had no post to whisk my complaints, for a single penny, to the remotest corners of the empire.

Written by the Reverend Sydney Smith in 1839, about changes in his lifetime. It is part of a longer list of important changes that had improved his life by the beginning of Queen Victoria's reign.

Source B

These men, photographed in the late 1880s, cleaned and disinfected London's streets. They were part of the new measures introduced by London's Board of Health.

A painting of London at sunset in 1884, by John O'Connor. Notice the horse-drawn trams instead of buses. They were introduced in 1860.

Activity

Look at the Discoveries and inventions box, and at the 1891 census on page 48. What jobs can you find that people could not have had in 1837?

Source D

An early motor car, photographed in 1895. People reacted to cars as they had to trains.

How did things change?

Things are always changing.

1 Read Source A and look at the information box. Think about the other changes discussed in Part Three of this book.

Sydney Smith was sure there had been many changes for the better in his life. Write a similar paragraph that Smith's son might have written in 1901.

2 Compare Source C with Source A on pages 16–17.
Have things changed in London?

3 Do you think that things were changing at the same rate all over Great Britain? Explain your answer.

INDEX

Conversion chart	
6d (old pennies)	= 2.4p
1s (shilling)	= 5p
10s	= 50p
20s	= £1
There were 12d to one shilling and 20s to £1.	
Cost of a loaf of bread:	
1842 – 5d	
1870 – 8d	
1895 – 5d	